Every Day Is Christmas

Other Books by Bradley Trevor Greive

Every Day Is Christmas

BRADLEY TREVOR GREIVE

**Andrews McMeel
Publishing, LLC**

Kansas City • Sydney • London

Every Day Is Christmas

Copyright © 2007, 2011 by The Lost Bear Company Pty. Ltd. All rights reserved. Printed in China.
No part of this book may be used or reproduced in any manner whatsoever without written permission except
in the case of reprints in the context of reviews.

Andrews McMeel Publishing, LLC
an Andrews McMeel Universal company
1130 Walnut Street, Kansas City, Missouri 64106

www.andrewsmcmeel.com

11 12 13 14 15 WKT 10 9 8 7 6 5 4 3 2 1

ISBN: 978-1-4494-1409-2

Library of Congress Control Number: 2007924479

www.andrewsmcmeel.com

Book design by Holly Ogden

Attention: Schools and Businesses

Andrews McMeel books are available at quantity discounts with bulk purchase for educational, business, or
sales promotional use. For information, please e-mail the Andrews McMeel Publishing Special Sales Department:
specialsales@amuniversal.com

Photo Credits

ALAMY/ TRI-SCAN (Australia) www.photosforme.com
AMANDA JONES (USA) www.amandajones.com
AUSCAPE (Australia) www.auscape.com.au
AUSTRAL (Australia) www.australphoto.com.au
CORBIS AUSTRALIA PTY LTD www.corbis.com
DANIEL J. COX / NATURAL EXPOSURES (USA) www.naturalexposures.com
GETTY IMAGES www.gettyimages.com
JUPITER IMAGES (Australia) www.jupiterimages.com.au
NATURE PICTURE LIBRARY (UK) www.naturepl.com
PHOTOLIBRARY (Australia) www.photolibrary.com
PREMIUM (Germany) www.premiumnatur.de
WILDLIGHT PHOTO AGENCY (Australia) www.wildlight.net

Detailed page credits for the remarkable photographers whose work appears in *Every Day Is Christmas*
and other books by Bradley Trevor Greive are freely available at www.btgstudios.com.

Acknowledgments

Ever since I was a little boy with a shiny face and a fistful of ill-gotten confectionary, I have looked forward to our family Christmas. Each year my mother would rally my sisters and me to decorate the tree, though I must confess my sisters did almost all the work while I would lie on the floor playing with the beautiful ornaments and figurines. My favorites were the Indian reindeer that had little mirrored pieces stitched to their glossy flanks. My father would sit on the sofa and make abstract observations that were no help to anyone who could be bothered to listen, and later one of the family pets would attack the tree and we would start all over again. It was heaven.

I have never missed a family Christmas gathering in my life, and I plan never to let that happen. Not that I was always home on December 25. During my years in the army and, more recently, with various international obligations, sometimes I was absent on this special day. But my family has always made the time for a special Christmas celebration together whether it was a week late or a month early—and I loved that.

In fact, it was our flexible family Christmas dates that first gave me the idea for this little book. In a rare moment of clarity I thought, hey, if *any day could be Christmas* then why can't *every day be Christmas*? The more I read about the history of the world's most important holiday, the more it made sense. We can and should celebrate the joys and values of Christmas with those we love far more often than once a year.

When you mention the word "Christmas," most selfish people immediately think of receiving gifts—I know I do. And some of the gifts I am most grateful for are the people who make my life as enjoyable as it is. I am so thankful for my wise, long-suffering editor in Kansas City, Christine Schillig, and Nerida Robinson, who fearlessly leads my team at BTG STUDIOS in Australia. I am also grateful to Mrs. Jacqueline Barr who, like a happy Christmas elf, always jumps in to help me get things done in Tasmania. I would be lost without these wonderful people.

Clearly this book would not be what it is without the many extraordinary photographers and image libraries throughout the world with whom I collaborate. I encourage everyone interested in superb professional photography to seek out their updated contact details posted at www.btgstudios.com.

Of course, in my world, the benevolent and jolly ambassador of Christmas is not a chubby old Laplander with a white beard but a buff Jewish gentleman with a glittering silver mustache—my longtime literary agent and dear friend, Albert J. Zuckerman of Writers House, New York.

I remember one cold December morning in Manhattan when we waded through several feet of snow and slush toward an uptown tennis club where I would endure our Christmas tradition of a crushing straight sets loss. As we passed the Christmas tree sellers dusting the snow off their stock for early commuters, Al stopped to admire a voluptuous fir and said, "Bradley, my boy, don't you think it curious that we take these beautiful trees into our homes only after they are already dying?" I had never considered this rather morbid thought before, and so I just stood there, shivering and slack-jawed, wondering how hard it would be to make a pair of snowshoes out of our tennis rackets. "My point is," he continued, "everything that is alive and beautiful about Christmas, Hanukkah, Kwanzaa, whatever, is in our hearts and homes already. The beautiful thing is that, for a time at least, we give this tree new life with the love in our hearts, just as we give life to everything that is beautiful in our world by sharing that love in our hearts."

With that, Al turned to the Christmas tree seller, paid for the best tree she had, and then stopped her from actually giving it to him. He gently put his hand on her arm and said, "Next year, cut down one less tree for me, okay?" We all shared a quiet smile, and then we went on our way.

Thank you, Sir Albert, for showing me that the beauty of Christmas is alive.

Every Day Is
Christmas

The wait is over!

At last, the Christmas spirit has completed the
twelve-month journey back to our hearts.

Listen as the midnight air is split crisply and sweetly by the
heavy tolling of large, ponderous church bells.

Taste the sugared wonders and delights that send even the most wooden tongues into quivering ecstasy.

Gaze upon the glittering bloom of decorations that transform
our streets and homes into a garden of stars.

For many, great feasting is the highlight, leaving them in a
state of pant-rending immobility, waistlines polished and straining
like sacks of Christmas pudding adrift at sea.

As homes fill with gifts, the nights drag on interminably for those
who struggle to contain the festive frenzy fizzing within, tossing and turning,
hoping their transgressions might be overlooked just this once.

Meanwhile, a select few "enjoy the honey-heavy dew of slumber" that only a genuinely clear conscience or premium legal representation can provide.

But no matter how much intoxicating seasonal excitement,
earnest yammering, radiant fluffery, and plastic decoration we indulge in,
these things do not explain the fundamental enduring joy of Christmas
or answer the one truly interesting question:

What does Christmas really mean today?

The answer, of course, can be found in the straw of the fabled Bethlehem stables some 2000 years ago. The birth of Jesus Christ was, in every meaningful way, the birth of hope. To this day, Christmas remains a joyful celebration of hope reborn for both Christians and non-Christians alike.

The way this manifests itself varies greatly from place to place
and culture to culture. While people in Europe and North America might
enjoy Christmas Eve amid legions of mitten-molded snowmen, 13

at the exact same time, many Australians and Africans
will celebrate while making sand angels at the beach.

Regardless of the many different interpretations and religious beliefs,
the simple, universal truth about the holiday season
is that billions of people, from all walks of life, look forward to
this time of year in a state of joyous wonderment.

After all, it is a truly magical time.

So magical that even folks who have been fixated on their own lot
now invest serious time thinking about what they can do
to brighten up someone else's life—a compete reversal
of the often maligned human condition.

And as if that weren't enough, cab drivers and truck drivers are suddenly polite and friendly, even in New York!

There are so many wonderful things to enjoy on the world's greatest holiday. For starters, Christmas *is* a holiday and for many that means a long overdue rest.

As the spirit revives, we have a chance to uncork the champagne
and celebrate life, love, and laughter in whatever ratio
that feels right, and legal, at the time.

Who can forget the joy of finding the perfect gift
for someone you adore?

Christmas means traditional carols and a host of holiday favorites
that bring back wonderful memories and make you want to sing out loud—
even when you know you shouldn't.

It means being drunk with joy and perhaps a little eggnog to boot.

It means an abundance of sincere *thank you*'s and *you're welcome*'s.

And as it has for more than a thousand years,
Christmas means togetherness.

Christmas is the best day of the year to observe and uphold the
true value of family. It reforges the lifelong bond between family members
and reminds them just how much they have in common,
regardless of where life has taken them.

"Hey, wait a minute. If *I* brought the brandy,
and *you* brought the brandy—then *who* brought the food?"

Of course, we can't forget the exchange of presents, which—like kissing—
is an extremely gratifying exercise for all parties but also involves
the exquisite agony of anticipation that makes it difficult
for people to hide their excitement.

Normally reserved folks resort to the "Christmas creep,"
sneaking quietly around the house at all hours to peek at the gifts
piling up beneath the Christmas tree to see which ones are theirs.

Watching people try to guess what is inside each gift-wrapped parcel
seems to disprove the existence of ESP.

Still, the act of gently shaking and jostling presents to ascertain their contents can be wickedly exciting, pleasantly confounding, and, just occasionally, enlightening.

At last the moment of revelation arrives, and there you are, enraptured to the point of rupture, face to face with that one special thing that you have yearned for every waking moment since last Christmas . . .

unless what you really wanted was a first edition of *Ulysses* by James Joyce, and maybe some nice body lotion with jojoba.

With everyone watching (and they are *all* watching), you now have to endure the seemingly endless and undignified horror of gallantly pretending that your gift was just what you were dreaming of.

There are many ways Christmas can lose its luster.
In fact, it can easily become all-consuming and very stressful.

Should you shop early and methodically for gifts or
race around at the last minute to save time?

What on earth do you buy for the person who has everything?

Did you remember to send out all the cards and
order the turkey and ham? Yikes!

Meanwhile, no matter where you go, you can't escape
that accursed album of Christmas songs sung by the latest
tone-deaf sixteen-year-old pop sensation.

Soon you have a headache that feels as if a hot thumbtack
has been slowly pressed into the back of your left eyeball,
but you've got to keep going.

Dash off to buy a Christmas tree,

quickly zip out and get wrapping paper and ribbon
before the best designs vanish,

screech over to the grocery store to get all the food, and then
do another thirteen hot laps of the mall in case you forgot somebody.
It wouldn't be so bad if you got frequent-flier miles for your feet.

Soon you're worn down and utterly exhausted, but you still haven't finished the first page of your ten-page list. You're starting to lose both your Christmas spirit and your will to live,

and now you feel a cold coming on.

Soon, too soon, the guests arrive. Quick, break out the fake smiles.
Time to exchange awkward kisses with thin-lipped relatives

and grit your teeth while generally absent uncles
roughhouse the small children under the bizarre illusion
that the poor little kids actually enjoy it.

Meanwhile, great-aunts and grandparents laugh so loud and violently at their
own feeble jokes they are in genuine danger of coughing up a kidney.

Then, the reaction to your carefully chosen gift is underwhelming.

"What do you mean, 'Batteries *not* included'?!"

Most people think that Christmas has become perversely overcommercialized, and it's hard to disagree.

It has become painfully expensive, too. Every step at the local mall bites deeper and deeper into your hard-earned savings. In Ireland, the average Christmas expenditure per person now exceeds $5,000!

Whatever seems to be the latest and greatest—*we must have it!*
Kids drive their parents mad demanding kittens they won't feed, games they
won't play, and dirt bikes they won't ride for more than a month.

And off we go, like a legion of credit-card-wielding zombies,

marching off happily to be chewed up and spat out by
a giant faceless monster of soulless consumerism.

I strongly suspect that the reason superintelligent, peace-loving beings from other galaxies have not made contact with us is because they have watched two old ladies choking each other over the last set of designer tea towels featuring seasonal motifs.

And God only knows what they think about the
gladiatorial spectacle of the January sales.

Nevertheless, malignant commercialization is merely a symptom.
The actual problem is that somehow, over time, the meaning of Christmas
has gotten all mixed up. The things that should be most important
no longer are. It's all backward.

If Christmas has started to smell bad to you, don't blame others for pooh-poohing the babe in a manger. Ask yourself, "Is it me?"

"It *is* me!"
Just like bad body odor, the source of most ills
is usually closer to home than you might want to believe.

Examine your own motivations and behavior, and be honest about your part in all of this. To some degree, we have brought this situation upon ourselves by buying into it.

It's worth making some changes so that we can enjoy
ourselves even more—after all, the Christmas season
was not supposed to be merely endured.

These wonder-filled days and sacred hours were meant be treasured.
Always.

Rigorous clinical tests show there is no inherent magic power in mistletoe or holly berries—only in our hearts.

So instead of knocking yourself out to deck the halls,

just let the spirit of Christmas come into your home—it's that simple.

And if you'd like some more free advice
about how to have a wonderful Christmas, here it is:

Be the star at the top of your tree.

By which I mean, become a Christmas ambassador
and take the spirit with you wherever you go.

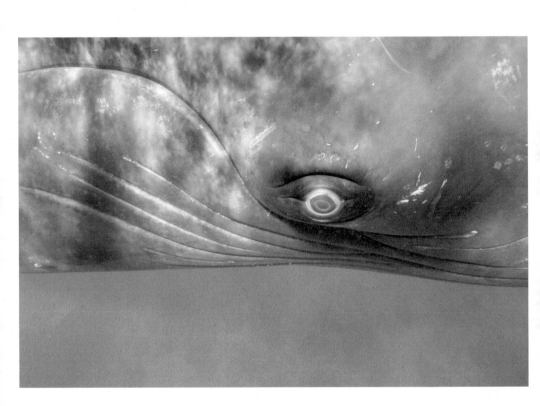

Imagine how you might react if the Creator, looking down upon us,
decided to send us an angel as a celestial messenger of Christmas
to grant us all one special wish.

Obviously you'd be entitled to freak out a little bit,

but when you had recovered from the shock, what question
would you ask, what one wish would you want granted by this
beautiful, pure manifestation of peace, hope, and love? Well, I can certainly
tell you what I *wouldn't* be asking . . .

"I wanna new cell phone, some diamond earrings, some new Nikes, and a mountain bike, and TiVo, and a Neiman Marcus charge card . . . and hey, how about one of big George's fat-free grills!"

Obviously we'd all be a lot happier if we spent less time whining about what we wanted and more time being thankful for the many good things we already enjoy.

There are very few things in life worth wishing for
beyond the health and happiness of our family and friends.
If you have that, you have it all.

We should be grateful that we have enough to eat—let alone have
the opportunity to indulge in delicious Christmas dinners.

We should be grateful that we are not alone in this world and that, especially at Christmastime, we are surrounded by those we love.

One thing to keep in mind is that Christmas Day is celebrated
at many different times from September to February, depending on various
customs and beliefs. In other words, an "ordinary day" *becomes* Christmas Day
by virtue of the meaning we give it, not because of any ironclad rule.
Therefore, why can't every day be Christmas?

Okay, not literally, or we'd all need weekly liver transplants.

But why not vest every day with at least some of the values
and highlights that make Christmas so much more exciting and uplifting
than the other 364 days of the year?

Remember, every day gives you a fresh start, so it doesn't really matter so much what happened the year, month, or day before. You can make things right today, and that's what counts.

There is often a fine line between a great day and a lousy day, Christmas or otherwise. A little luck certainly helps, but preparation

and imagination always make the biggest difference.

You don't have to reinvent the wheel—just add a little pizzazz to your routine.
Wear that outfit you thought was too wild for the office,

and, unless your medical alert bracelet warns you otherwise,
why not try something for lunch or dinner that you wouldn't normally eat?

With a little bit of creative effort and a sense of humor, you'll soon realize that all manner of Christmas delights are available every day.

The next step is to pass this on to your family,
your friends, and your colleagues.

Not only is this the true spirit of Christmas at its best but,
with the exception of chicken pox, just about everything is more enjoyable
when you have someone to share it with.

At the end of the day we are all in this together.

So on this or any day, why not at least try to stop
making life hard for each other?

Share the love, baby!

If people abuse you, shrug it off and stun them with genuine good wishes. They will feel worse, and you will feel better. It's a win-win!

Christmas is all about making sacrifices—traveling way out of your comfort zone to touch the lives of others in the belief that you can make a difference.

And not just family and friends.

I also mean people you would never normally come in contact with.

To get the most out of Christmas, we just have to break through
the "me, me, me" barrier.

Put yourself in someone else's shoes for a while and think of what you
could do to make them feel loved, appreciated, and joyful.

And hey, if it doesn't work out, you will then know all their weaknesses in order to crush them once and for all, heh, heh, heh!
But I digress.

The first thing to remember is that none of this should cost a fortune.

In fact, sometimes it costs nothing at all. Even the smallest gesture can mean an enormous amount.

Who has not been moved to tears of joy by a simple card,

an unexpected phone call,

or a warm hug?

The meaning of Christmas is to give of yourself—to open up the joy in your heart and share it generously. If you do this properly, then every day will feel like . . . well, like Christmas.

I'm not saying you'll run around screaming, "Joy to the World!" at the top of your lungs. That would only terrify the very old and the very young and cause small animals to scatter into the path of oncoming traffic.

If you can just tiptoe a little out of your way—not even a full extra mile,
just a few inches more each day—you will certainly have more fun
and so will everyone who crosses your path.

Then, when you greet them with a smile and say, "Hi!"

you'll really be saying, "Merry Christmas!"

"Mewwy Cwithmath!"

"Me-rry Christ-mas!"

"MERRRRRY CHRISTMASSSSS!"

Pick it up and give it a shake—
you never know what good things might come out of it.

So don't just sit there. The best day of the year is about to begin.

Since the debut of his international best-seller *The Blue Day Book*, Bradley Trevor Greive has become a household name in more than 105 countries. A former Australian paratrooper, BTG left the army to pursue more creative misadventures. He has been bitten by wild monkeys and rabid bats and was accepted into Russia's cosmonaut training program—though those incidents were hopefully unrelated. BTG spends most of his time in a tiny Tasmanian hamlet.

Bradley Trevor Greive loves animals and proudly supports the Taronga Foundation. To find out how you too can easily make a difference by becoming a zoo parent or making a donation toward vitally important research and breeding programs, visit the Taronga Foundation Web site: www.tarongafoundation.org

(P.S. Merry Christmas!)